DOG POEMS

DOG
POEMS

By the World's Greatest Poets

First published in 2019 by Serpent's Tail,
an imprint of Profile Books Ltd
29 Cloth Fair
London
EC1A 7NN
www.serpentstail.com

10 9 8 7 6 5 4 3 2

Collection originally edited by Leonora Craig Cohen

Designed and typeset by sue@lambledesign.demon.co.uk

Printed and bound in Great Britain by CPI Group (UK) Ltd,
Croydon CR0 4YY

ISBN 978 1 78816 365 1
eISBN 978 1 78283 620 9

Contents

To Flush, My Dog

Loving friend, the gift of one,
Who, her own true faith, hath run,
Through thy lower nature ;
Be my benediction said
With my hand upon thy head,
Gentle fellow-creature !

Like a lady's ringlets brown,
Flow thy silken ears adown
Either side demurely,
Of thy silver-suited breast
Shining out from all the rest
Of thy body purely.

Darkly brown thy body is,
Till the sunshine, striking this,
Alchemize its dulness, —
When the sleek curls manifold
Flash all over into gold,
With a burnished fulness.

Underneath my stroking hand,
Startled eyes of hazel bland
Kindling, growing larger, —

Up thou leapest with a spring,
Full of prank and curvetting,
Leaping like a charger.

Leap ! thy broad tail waves a light ;
Leap ! thy slender feet are bright,
Canopied in fringes.
Leap — those tasselled ears of thine
Flicker strangely, fair and fine,
Down their golden inches.

Yet, my pretty sportive friend,
Little is 't to such an end
That I praise thy rareness !
Other dogs may be thy peers
Haply in these drooping ears,
And this glossy fairness.

But of thee it shall be said,
This dog watched beside a bed
Day and night unweary, —
Watched within a curtained room,
Where no sunbeam brake the gloom
Round the sick and dreary.

Roses, gathered for a vase,
In that chamber died apace,
Beam and breeze resigning —
This dog only, waited on,
Knowing that when light is gone,
Love remains for shining.

Other dogs in thymy dew
Tracked the hares and followed through
Sunny moor or meadow —
This dog only, crept and crept
Next a languid cheek that slept,
Sharing in the shadow.

Other dogs of loyal cheer
Bounded at the whistle clear,
Up the woodside hieing —
This dog only, watched in reach
Of a faintly uttered speech,
Or a louder sighing.

And if one or two quick tears
Dropped upon his glossy ears,
Or a sigh came double, —
Up he sprang in eager haste,
Fawning, fondling, breathing fast,
In a tender trouble.

And this dog was satisfied,
If a pale thin hand would glide,
Down his dewlaps sloping, —
Which he pushed his nose within,
After, — platforming his chin
On the palm left open.

This dog, if a friendly voice
Call him now to blyther choice
Than such chamber-keeping,
Come out ! ' praying from the door, —
Presseth backward as before,
Up against me leaping.

Therefore to this dog will I,
Tenderly not scornfully,
Render praise and favour !
With my hand upon his head,
Is my benediction said
Therefore, and for ever.

And because he loves me so,
Better than his kind will do
Often, man or woman,
Give I back more love again
Than dogs often take of men, —
Leaning from my Human.

Blessings on thee, dog of mine,
Pretty collars make thee fine,
Sugared milk make fat thee !
Pleasures wag on in thy tail —
Hands of gentle motion fail
Nevermore, to pat thee !

Downy pillow take thy head,
Silken coverlid bestead,
Sunshine help thy sleeping !
No fly 's buzzing wake thee up —
No man break thy purple cup,
Set for drinking deep in.

Whiskered cats arointed flee —
Sturdy stoppers keep from thee
Cologne distillations ;
Nuts lie in thy path for stones,
And thy feast-day macaroons
Turn to daily rations !

Mock I thee, in wishing weal ? —
Tears are in my eyes to feel
Thou art made so straightly,
Blessing needs must straighten too, —
Little canst thou joy or do,
Thou who lovest greatly.

Yet be blessed to the height
Of all good and all delight
Pervious to thy nature, —
Only loved beyond that line,
With a love that answers thine,
Loving fellow-creature !

Every Dog's Story

I have a bed, my very own.
It's just my size.
And sometimes I like to sleep alone
with dreams inside my eyes.

But sometimes dreams are dark and wild and creepy
and I wake and am afraid, though I don't know why.
But I'm no longer sleepy
and too slowly the hours go by.

So I climb on the bed where the light of the moon
is shining on your face
and I know it will be morning soon.

Everybody needs a safe place.

On the Collar of a Dog

I am his highness's dog at Kew;
Pray tell me, sir, whose dog are you?

VINCENT STARRETT

Oracle of the Dog

Only the dog knows why the moon
Floats down the night; his raucous tune
Is urgent with the thing he fears,
But falls on unbelieving ears.
If we had only learned to speak
The tongue of dogs instead of Greek,
We should be better schooled to fight
The spells and portents of the night,
Now at the coming of the dark
Young fools adrift in street and park
Yield to an epidemic swoon,
Abuse the dog and praise the moon.

An Introduction to Dogs

The dog is man's best friend.
He has a tail on one end.
Up in front he has teeth.
And four legs underneath.
Dogs like to bark.
They like it best after dark.
They not only frighten prowlers away
But also hold the sandman at bay.
A dog that is indoors
To be let out implores.
You let him out and what then?
He wants back in again.
Dogs display reluctance and wrath
If you try to give them a bath.
They bury bones in hideaways
And half the time they trot sideways.
Dogs in the country have fun.
They run and run and run.
But in the city this species
Is dragged around on leashes.
Dogs are upright as a steeple
And much more loyal than people.
Well people may be reprehensibler
But that's probably because they are sensibler.

Epitaph to a Dog

Near this Spot
are deposited the Remains of one
who possessed Beauty without Vanity,
Strength without Insolence,
Courage without Ferosity,
and all the virtues of Man without his Vices.
This praise, which would be unmeaning Flattery
if inscribed over human Ashes,
is but a just tribute to the Memory of
BOATSWAIN, a DOG,
who was born in Newfoundland May 1803
and died at Newstead Nov. 18th, 1808.

When some proud Son of Man returns to Earth,
Unknown to Glory but upheld by Birth,
The sculptor's art exhausts the pomp of woe,
And storied urns record who rests below:
When all is done, upon the Tomb is seen
Not what he was, but what he should have been.
But the poor Dog, in life the firmest friend,
The first to welcome, foremost to defend,
Whose honest heart is still his Master's own,
Who labours, fights, lives, breathes for him alone,
Unhonour'd falls, unnotic'd all his worth,

Deny'd in heaven the Soul he held on earth:
While man, vain insect! hopes to be forgiven,
And claims himself a sole exclusive heaven.
Oh man! thou feeble tenant of an hour,
Debas'd by slavery, or corrupt by power,
Who knows thee well, must quit thee with disgust,
Degraded mass of animated dust!
Thy love is lust, thy friendship all a cheat,
Thy tongue hypocrisy, thy heart deceit!
By nature vile, ennobled but by name,
Each kindred brute might bid thee blush for shame.
Ye! who behold perchance this simple urn,
Pass on, it honors none you wish to mourn.
To mark a friend's remains these stones arise;
I never knew but one – and here he lies.

STEVIE SMITH

O Pug!

To the Brownes' pug dog, on my lap, in their car,
coming home from Norfolk.

O Pug, some people do not like you,
But I like you,
Some people say you do not breathe, you snore,
I don't mind,
One person says he is always conscious of your
    behind,
Is that your fault?

Your own people love you,
All the people in the family that owns you
Love you: Good pug, they cry, Happy pug,
Pug-come-for-a-walk.

You are an old dog now
And in all your life
You have never had cause for a moment's anxiety,
Yet,
In those great eyes of yours,
Those liquid and protuberant orbs,
Lies the shadow of immense insecurity. There
Panic walks.

Yes, yes, I know,
When your mistress is with you,
When your master
Takes you upon his lap,
Just then, for a moment,
Almost you are not frightened.

But at heart you are frightened, you always
        have been.

O Pug, obstinate old nervous breakdown,
In the midst of so much love,
And such comfort,
Still to feel unsafe and be afraid,

How one's heart goes out to you!

MARCHETTE CHUTE

My Dog

His nose is short and scrubby;
His ears hang rather low;
And he always brings the stick back
No matter how far you throw,

He gets spanked rather often
For things he shouldn't do,
Like lying-on-beds, and barking,
And eating up shoes when they're new

He always wants to be going
Where he isn't supposed to go.
He tracks up the house when it's snowing –
Oh, puppy, I love you so

To A Lady With An Unruly And Ill-Mannered Dog Who Bit Several Persons Of Importance

Your dog is not a dog of grace;
He does not wag the tail or beg;
He bit Miss Dickson in the face;
He bit a Bailie in the leg.

What tragic choices such a dog
Presents to visitor or friend!
Outside there is the Glasgow fog;
Within, a hydrophobic end.

Yet some relief even terror brings,
For when our life is cold and gray
We waste our strength on little things,
And fret our puny souls away.

A snarl! A scruffle round the room!
A sense that Death is drawing near!
And human creatures reassume
The elemental robe of fear.

So when my colleague makes his moan
Of careless cooks, and warts, and debt,
– Enlarge his views, restore his tone,
And introduce him to your Pet!

CATHRYN ESSINGER

My Dog Practices Geometry

I do not understand the poets who tell me
that I should not personify. Every morning
the willow auditions for a new role

outside my bedroom window – today she is
Clytemnestra; yesterday a Southern Belle,
lost in her own melodrama, sinking on her skirts.

Nor do I like the mathematicians who tell me
I cannot say, 'The zinnias are counting on their
fingers,' or 'The dog is practicing her geometry,'

even though every day I watch her using
the yard's big maple as the apex of a triangle
from which she bisects the circumference

of the lawn until she finds the place where
the rabbit has escaped, or the squirrel upped
the ante by climbing into a new Euclidian plane.

She stumbles across the lawn, eyes pulling
her feet along, gaze fixed on a rodent working
the maze of the oak as if it were his own invention,

her feet tangling in the roots of trees, and tripping,
yes, even over themselves, until I go out to assist,
by pointing at the squirrel, and repeating, 'There!

There!' But instead of following my outstretched
arm to the crown of the tree, where the animal is
now lounging under a canopy of leaves,

catching its breath, charting its next escape,
she looks to my mouth, eager to read my lips,
confident that I – who can bring her home

from across the field with a word, who
can speak for the willow and the zinnia –
can surely charm a squirrel down from a tree.

Roads

I know a country laced with roads,
They join the hills and they span the brooks,
They weave like a shuttle between broad fields,
And slide discreetly through hidden nooks.
They are canopied like a Persian dome
And carpeted with orient dyes.
They are myriad-voiced, and musical,
And scented with happiest memories.
O Winding roads that I know so well,
Every twist and turn, every hollow and hill!
They are set in my heart to a pulsing tune
Gay as a honey-bee humming in June.
'T is the rhythmic beat of a horse's feet
And the pattering paws of a sheep-dog bitch;
'T is the creaking trees, and the singing breeze,
And the rustle of leaves in the road-side ditch.

A cow in a meadow shakes her bell
And the notes cut sharp through the autumn air,
Each chattering brook bears a fleet of leaves
Their cargo the rainbow, and just now where
The sun splashed bright on the road ahead
A startled rabbit quivered and fled.
O Uphill roads and roads that dip down!

You curl your sun-spattered length along,
And your march is beaten into a song
By the softly ringing hoofs of a horse
And the panting breath of the dogs I love.
The pageant of Autumn follows its course
And the blue sky of Autumn laughs above.

And the song and the country become as one,
I see it as music, I hear it as light;
Prismatic and shimmering, trembling to tone,
The land of desire, my soul's delight.
And always it beats in my listening ears
With the gentle thud of a horse's stride,
With the swift-falling steps of many dogs,
Following, following at my side.
O Roads that journey to fairyland!
Radiant highways whose vistas gleam,
Leading me on, under crimson leaves,
To the opaline gates of the Castles of Dream.

Man and Dog

Who's this – alone with stone and sky?
It's only my old dog and I –
It's only him; it's only me;
Alone with stone and grass and tree.

What share we most – we two together?
Smells, and awareness of the weather.
What is it makes us more than dust?
My trust in him; in me his trust.

Here's anyhow one decent thing
That life to man and dog can bring;
One decent thing, remultiplied
Till earth's last dog and man have died.

Pink Dog

The sun is blazing and the sky is blue.
Umbrellas clothe the beach in every hue.
Naked, you trot across the avenue.

Oh, never have I seen a dog so bare!
Naked and pink, without a single hair ...
Startled, the passersby draw back and stare.

Of course they're mortally afraid of rabies.
You are not mad; you have a case of scabies
but look intelligent. Where are your babies?

(A nursing mother, by those hanging teats.)
In what slum have you hidden them, poor bitch,
while you go begging, living by your wits?

Didn't you know? It's been in all the papers,
to solve this problem, how they deal with beggars?
They take and throw them in the tidal rivers.

Yes, idiots, paralytics, parasites
go bobbing in the ebbing sewage, nights
out in the suburbs, where there are no lights.

If they do this to anyone who begs,
drugged, drunk, or sober, with or without legs,
what would they do to sick, four-legged dogs?

In the cafés and on the sidewalk corners
the joke is going round that all the beggars
who can afford them now wear life preservers.

In your condition you would not be able
even to float, much less to dog-paddle.
Now look, the practical, the sensible

solution is to wear a fantasía.
Tonight you simply can't afford to be a-
n eyesore ... But no one will ever see a

dog in máscara this time of year.
Ash Wednesday'll come but Carnival is here.
What sambas can you dance? What will you wear?

They say that Carnival's degenerating
– radios, Americans, or something,
have ruined it completely. They're just talking.

Carnival is always wonderful!
A depilated dog would not look well.
Dress up! Dress up and dance at Carnival!

Running through the grey-eyed dawn
with last night's trash in mind,
the brown dog scuttles
through fluted gates
while birds sing on above the world
about a bit of fallen cheese,
the shish kebob he ate
and all the vagaries of plates
that wait for him at home.

DOROTHY PARKER

Verse for a Certain Dog

Such glorious faith as fills your limpid eyes,
Dear little friend of mine, I never knew.
All-innocent are you, and yet all-wise.
(For Heaven's sake, stop worrying that shoe!)
You look about, and all you see is fair;
This mighty globe was made for you alone.
Of all the thunderous ages, you're the heir.
(Get off the pillow with that dirty bone!)

A skeptic world you face with steady gaze;
High in young pride you hold your noble head,
Gayly you meet the rush of roaring days.
(Must you eat puppy biscuit on the bed?)
Lancelike your courage, gleaming swift and strong,
Yours the white rapture of a winged soul,
Yours is a spirit like a Mayday song.
(God help you, if you break the goldfish bowl!)

'Whatever is, is good' – your gracious creed.
You wear your joy of living like a crown.
Love lights your simplest act, your every deed.
(Drop it, I tell you – put that kitten down!)

You are God's kindliest gift of all – a friend.
Your shining loyalty unflecked by doubt,
You ask but leave to follow to the end.
(Couldn't you wait until I took you out?)

Unfinished Landscape With A Dog

Not much of a dog yet,
that smudge in the distance, beyond the reach

of focus. It's just an impressionist
gesture, a guess. From the edge of the clearing,
    the farmhouse
materializes, settles

into wall & stone. The water,
making the surface

of the stream, makes
reflections. So why shouldn't the dog

accept limits, become

a figure? Is it like the girl who sits
in the hall closet and says she's not
hiding? She's inside –

listening without the burden
of sight, letting locations
release hold. Out of body,
they seem lighter: her parents' voices no longer

hooked to their mouths. They seem
cleaner. Even the electric can opener;
the sounds of children

that rise from the yard, and fall; the opening
window, these are no longer

effects, things expected
of a subject and verb. The world anyhow is too
straightforward.

Maybe the dog
does not want to be a dog, does not want
to be turned into landscape

but to remain in the beginning, placeless:

with the wind opening, the wind
a vowel, and the stars and waters
that flash, recoil, and retch

unnamed as yet, unformed, unfound.

ROBINSON JEFFERS

The House Dog's Grave

I've changed my ways a little; I cannot now
Run with you in the evenings along the shore,
Except in a kind of dream; and you,
If you dream a moment,
You see me there.

So leave awhile the paw-marks on the front door
Where I used to scratch to go out or in,
And you'd soon open; leave on the kitchen floor
The marks of my drinking-pan.

I cannot lie by your fire as I used to do
On the warm stone,
Nor at the foot of your bed; no,
All the nights through I lie alone.

But your kind thought has laid me less than six feet
Outside your window where firelight so often plays,
And where you sit to read,
And I fear often grieving for me,
Every night your lamplight lies on my place.

You, man and woman, live so long, it is hard
To think of you ever dying.

A little dog would get tired, living so long.
I hope that when you are lying
Under the ground like me your lives will appear
As good and joyful as mine.

No, dears, that's too much hope:
You are not so well cared for as I have been.
And never have known the passionate undivided
Fidelities that I knew.
Your minds are perhaps too active, too
    many-sided ...
But to me you were true.

You were never masters, but friends. I was
    your friend.
I loved you well, and was loved. Deep love endures
To the end and far past the end. If this is my end,
I am not lonely. I am not afraid. I am still yours.

WILLIAM SHAKESPEARE

from *Macbeth*

Ay, in the catalogue ye go for men,
As hounds and greyhounds, mongrels,
　　spaniels, curs,
Shoughs, water-rugs, and demi-wolves are clept
All by the name of dogs. The valued file
Distinguishes the swift, the slow, the subtle,
The housekeeper, the hunter, every one
According to the gift which bounteous nature
Hath in him closed, whereby he does receive
Particular addition, from the bill
That writes them all alike. And so of men.
Now, if you have a station in the file,
Not i' th' worst rank of manhood, say 't,
And I will put that business in your bosoms,
Whose execution takes your enemy off,
Grapples you to the heart and love of us,
Who wear our health but sickly in his life,
Which in his death were perfect.

Tom's Little Dog

Tom told his dog called Tim to beg,
And up at once he sat,
His two clear amber eyes fixed fast,
His haunches on his mat.
Tom poised a lump of sugar on
His nose; then, 'Trust!' says he;
Stiff as a guardsman sat his Tim;
Never a hair stirred he.

'Paid for!' says Tom; and in a trice
Up jerked that moist black nose;
A snap of teeth, a crunch, a munch,
And down the sugar goes!

Of The Awefull Battle Of The Pekes And The Pollicles

*Together With Some Account Of The Participation
Of The Pugs And The Poms, And The Intervention
Of The Great Rumpuscat*

The Pekes and the Pollicles, everyone knows,
Are proud and implacable passionate foes;
It is always the same, wherever one goes.
And the Pugs and the Poms, although most
    people say
That they do not like fighting, will often display
Every symptom of wanting to join in the fray.
And they
       Bark bark bark bark
       Bark bark BARK BARK
      Until you can hear them all over the Park.

Now on the occasion of which I shall speak
Almost nothing had happened for nearly a week
(And that's a long time for a Pol or a Peke).
The big Police Dog was away from his beat –
I don't know the reason, but most people think
He'd slipped into the Bricklayer's Arms for a drink –

And no one at all was about on the street
When a Peke and a Pollicle happened to meet.
They did not advance, or exactly retreat,
But they glared at each other and scraped their
    hind feet,
And started to
        Bark bark bark bark
        Bark bark BARK BARK
    Until you could hear them all over the Park.

Now the Peke, although people may say what
    they please,
Is no British Dog, but a Heathen Chinese.
And so all the Pekes, when they heard the uproar,
Some came to the window, some came to the door;
There were surely a dozen, more likely a score.
And together they started to grumble and wheeze
In their huffery-snuffery Heathen Chinese.
But a terrible din is what Pollicles like,
for your Pollicle Dog is a dour Yorkshire tyke,
And his braw Scottish cousins are snappers
    and biters,
And every dog-jack of them notable fighters;
And so they stepped out, with their pipers in order,
Playing When the Blue Bonnets Came Over
    the Border.

Then the Pugs and the Poms held no longer aloof,
But some from the balcony, some from the roof,
Joined in
To the din
With a

      Bark bark bark bark
      Bark bark BARK BARK
   Until you could hear them all over the Park.

Now when these bold heroes together assembled,
The traffic all stopped, and the Underground
    trembled,
And some of the neighbours were so much afraid
That they started to ring up the Fire Brigade.
When suddenly, up from a small basement flat,
Why who should stalk out but the GREAT
    RUMPUSCAT.
His eyes were like fireballs fearfully blazing,
He gave a great yawn, and his jaws were amazing;
And when he looked out through the bars of
    the area,
You never saw anything fiercer or hairier.
And what with the glare of his eyes and his
    yawning,
The Pekes and the Pollicles quickly took warning.

He looked at the sky and he gave a great leap –
And they every last one of them scattered like sheep.

And when the Police Dog returned to his beat,
There wasn't a single one left in the street.

Dog

The dog trots freely in the street
and sees reality
and the things he sees
are bigger than himself
and the things he sees
are his reality
Drunks in doorways
Moons on trees
The dog trots freely thru the street
and the things he sees
are smaller than himself
Fish on newsprint
Ants in holes
Chickens in Chinatown windows
their heads a block away
The dog trots freely in the street
and the things he smells
smell something like himself
The dog trots freely in the street
past puddles and babies
cats and cigars
poolrooms and policemen
He doesn't hate cops
He merely has no use for them

and he goes past them
and past the dead cows hung up whole
in front of the San Francisco Meat Market
He would rather eat a tender cow
than a tough policeman
though either might do
And he goes past the Romeo Ravioli Factory
and past Coit's Tower
and past Congressman Doyle
He's afraid of Coit's Tower
but he's not afraid of Congressman Doyle
although what he hears is very discouraging
very depressing
very absurd
to a sad young dog like himself
to a serious dog like himself
But he has his own free world to live in
His own fleas to eat
He will not be muzzled
Congressman Doyle is just another
fire hydrant
to him
The dog trots freely in the street
and has his own dog's life to live
and to think about
and to reflect upon

touching and tasting and testing everything
investigating everything
without benefit of perjury
a real realist
with a real tale to tell
and a real tail to tell it with
a real live
                barking
                        democratic dog
engaged in real
                free enterprise
with something to say
                        about ontology
something to say
                about reality
                        and how to see it
                                and how to hear it
with his head cocked sideways
                        at streetcorners
as if he is just about to have
                        his picture taken
                                for Victor Records
                listening for
                        His Master's Voice
                and looking
                        like a living questionmark
                                into the

great gramophone
of puzzling existence
with its wondrous hollow horn
which always seems
just about to spout forth
some Victorious answer
to everything

CECIL DAY-LEWIS

Sheepdog Trials in Hyde Park

A shepherd stands at one end of the arena.
Five sheep are unpenned at the other. His dog
    runs out
In a curve to behind them, fetches them straight
    to the shepherd,
Then drives the flock round a triangular course
Through a couple of gates and back to his master:
    two
Must be sorted there from the flock, then all
    five penned.
Gathering, driving away, shedding and penning
Are the plain words for the miraculous game.

An abstract game. What can the sheepdog make
    of such
Simplified terrain? – no hills, dales, bogs,
    walls, tracks,
Only a quarter-mile plain of grass, dumb crowds
Like crowds on hoardings around it, and
    behind them
Traffic or mounds of lovers and children playing.
Well, the dog is no landscape-fancier: his
    whole concern

Is with his master's whistle, and of course
With the flock – sheep are sheep anywhere for him.

The sheep are the chanciest element. Why, for
    instance,
Go through this gate when there's on either side
    of it
No wall or hedge but huge and viable space?
Why not eat the grass instead of being pushed
    around it?
Like a blob of quicksilver on a tilting board
The flock erratically runs, dithers, breaks up,
Is reassembled: their ruling idea is the dog;
And behind the dog, though they know it not yet,
    is a shepherd.

The shepherd knows that time is of the essence
But haste calamitous. Between dog and sheep
There is always an ideal distance, a perfect angle;
But these are constantly varying, so the man
Should anticipate each move through the dog,
    his medium.
The shepherd is the brain behind the dog's brain,
But his control of dog, like dog's of sheep,
Is never absolute – that's the beauty of it.

For beautiful it is. The guided missiles,
The black-and-white angels follow each quirk
      and jink of
The evasive sheep, play grandmother's-steps
      behind them,
Freeze to the ground, or leap to head off a straggler
Almost before it knows that it wants to stray,
As if radar-controlled. But they are not machines –
You can feel them feeling mastery, doubt, chagrin:
Machines don't frolic when their job is done.

What's needfully done in the solitude of
      sheep-runs –
Those rough, real tasks become this stylized game,
A demonstration of intuitive wit
Kept natural by the saving grace of error.
To lift, to fetch, to drive, to shed, to pen
Are acts I recognize, with all they mean
Of shepherding the unruly, for a kind of
Controlled woolgathering is my work too.

PABLO NERUDA

A Dog Has Died

My dog has died.
I buried him in the garden
next to a rusted old machine.

Some day I'll join him right there,
but now he's gone with his shaggy coat,
his bad manners and his cold nose,
and I, the materialist, who never believed
in any promised heaven in the sky
for any human being,
I believe in a heaven I'll never enter.
Yes, I believe in a heaven for all dogdom
where my dog waits for my arrival
waving his fan-like tail in friendship.

Ai, I'll not speak of sadness here on earth,
of having lost a companion
who was never servile.
His friendship for me, like that of a porcupine
withholding its authority,
was the friendship of a star, aloof,
with no more intimacy than was called for,
with no exaggerations:
he never climbed all over my clothes

filling me full of his hair or his mange,
he never rubbed up against my knee
like other dogs obsessed with sex.

No, my dog used to gaze at me,
paying me the attention I need,
the attention required
to make a vain person like me understand
that, being a dog, he was wasting time,
but, with those eyes so much purer than mine,
he'd keep on gazing at me
with a look that reserved for me alone
all his sweet and shaggy life,
always near me, never troubling me,
and asking nothing.

Ai, how many times have I envied his tail
as we walked together on the shores of the sea
in the lonely winter of Isla Negra
where the wintering birds filled the sky
and my hairy dog was jumping about
full of the voltage of the sea's movement:
my wandering dog, sniffing away
with his golden tail held high,
face to face with the ocean's spray.

Joyful, joyful, joyful,
as only dogs know how to be happy
with only the autonomy
of their shameless spirit.

There are no good-byes for my dog who has died,
and we don't now and never did lie to each other.

So now he's gone and I buried him,
and that's all there is to it.

Translated by Alfred Yankauer

Beagles

that boxing day morning, I would hear the familiar,
far-off gowls and gulders,
over keenaghan and aughanlig
of a pack of beagles, old dogs disinclined to
    chase a car
suddenly quite unlike

themselves, pups coming helter-skelter
across the ploughlands with all the chutzpah
    of veterans
of the trenches, their slate-greys, cinnamons, liver-
browns, lemons, rusts and violets

turning and twisting, unseen, across the fields,
their gowls and gulders turning and twisting
    after the
twists and turns
of the great hare who had just now sauntered
    into the
yard where I stood on tiptoe

astride my new Raleigh cycle,
his demeanour somewhat louche, somewhat
lackadaisical

under the circumstances, what with him
    standing on
tiptoe

as if to mimic me, standing almost as tall as I,
    looking
as if he might for a moment put
himself in my place, thinking better of it,
    sloping off
behind the lorry bed.

PAUL ZIMMER

Dog Music

Amongst dogs are listeners and singers.
My big dog sang with me so purely,
puckering her ruffled lips into an O,
beginning with small, swallowing sounds
like Coltrane musing, then rising to power
and resonance, gulping air to continue –
her passion and sense of flawless form –
singing not with me, but for the art of dogs.
We joined in many fine songs – 'Stardust,'
'Naima,' 'The Trout,' 'My Rosary,' 'Perdido.'
She was a great master and died young,
leaving me with unrelieved grief,
her talents known to only a few.

Now I have a small dog who does not sing,
but listens with discernment, requiring
skill and spirit in my falsetto voice.
I sing her name and words of love
andante, con brio, vivace, adagio.
Sometimes she is so moved she turns
to place a paw across her snout,
closes her eyes, sighing like a girl
I held and danced with years ago.

But I am a pretender to dog music.
The true strains rise only from
the rich, red chambers of a canine heart,
these melodies best when the moon is up,
listeners and singers together or
apart, beyond friendship and anger,
far from any human imposter –
ballads of long nights lifting
to starlight, songs of bones, turds,
conquests, hunts, smells, rankings,
things settled long before our birth.

Lone Dog

I'm a lean dog, a keen dog, a wild dog, and lone;
I'm a rough dog, a tough dog, hunting on my own;
I'm a bad dog, a mad dog, teasing silly sheep;
I love to sit and bay the moon, to keep fat souls
    from sleep.

I'll never be a lap dog, licking dirty feet,
A sleek dog, a meek dog, cringing for my meat,
Not for me the fireside, the well-filled plate,
But shut door, and sharp stone, and cuff and kick,
    and hate.

Not for me the other dogs, running by my side,
Some have run a short while, but none of them
    would bide.
O mine is still the lone trail, the hard trail, the best,
Wide wind, and wild stars, and hunger of the quest!

Yoko

All today I lie in the bottom of the wardrobe
feeling low but sometimes getting up
to moodily lumber across rooms
and lap from the toilet bowl, it is so sultry
and then I hear the noise of firecrackers again
all New York is jaggedy with firecrackers today
and I go back to the wardrobe gloomy
trying to void my mind of them.
I am confused, I feel loose and unfitted.

At last deep in the stairwell I hear a tread,
it is him, my leader, my love.
I run to the door and listen to his approach.
Now I can smell him, what a good man he is,
I love it when he has the sweat of work on him,
as he enters I yodel with happiness,
I throw my body up against his, I try to lick his lips,
I care about him more than anything.

After we eat we go for a walk to the piers.
I leap into the standing warmth, I plunge into
the combination of old and new smells.
Here on a garbage can at the bottom, so interesting,

what sister or brother I wonder left this message
	I sniff.
I too piss there, and go on.
Here a hydrant there a pole
here's a smell I left yesterday, well that's
disappointing
but I piss there anyway, and go on.

I investigate so much that in the end
it is for form's sake only, only a drop comes out.

I investigate tar and rotten sandwiches, everything,
	and go on.

And here a dried old turd, so interesting
so old, so dry, yet so subtle and mellow.
I can place it finely, I really appreciate it,
a gold distant smell like packed autumn leaves
	in winter
reminding me how what is rich and fierce
	when excreted
becomes weathered and mild
			but always interesting
and reminding me of what I have to do.

My leader looks on and expresses his approval.

I sniff it well and later I sniff the air well
a wind is meeting us after the close July day
rain is getting near too but first the wind.
Joy, joy,
being outside with you, active, investigating it all,
with bowels emptied, feeling your approval
and then running on, the big fleet Yoko,
my body in its excellent black coat never lets
    me down,
returning to you (as I always will, you know that)
and now
        filling myself out with myself, no longer
            confused,
my panting pushing apart my black lips,
    but unmoving,
I stand with you braced against the wind.

THOMAS HARDY

A Popular Personage at Home

'I live here: "Wessex" is my name:
I am a dog known rather well:
I guard the house but how that came
To be my whim I cannot tell.

'With a leap and a heart elate I go
At the end of an hour's expectancy
To take a walk of a mile or so
With the folk I let live here with me.

'Along the path, amid the grass
I sniff, and find out rarest smells
For rolling over as I pass
The open fields toward the dells.

'No doubt I shall always cross this sill,
And turn the corner, and stand steady,
Gazing back for my Mistress till
She reaches where I have run already,

'And that this meadow with its brook,
And bulrush, even as it appears
As I plunge by with hasty look,
Will stay the same a thousand years.'

Thus 'Wessex.' But a dubious ray
At times informs his steadfast eye,
Just for a trice, as though to say,
'Yet, will this pass, and pass shall I?'

DYLAN THOMAS

Song of the Mischievous Dog

There are many who say that a dog has its day,
And a cat has a number of lives;
There are others who think that a lobster is pink,
And that bees never work in their hives.
There are fewer, of course, who insist that a horse
Has a horn and two humps on its head,
And a fellow who jests that a mare can build nests
Is as rare as a donkey that's red.
Yet in spite of all this, I have moments of bliss,
For I cherish a passion for bones,
And though doubtful of biscuit, I'm willing
    to risk it,
And I love to chase rabbits and stones.
But my greatest delight is to take a good bite
At a calf that is plump and delicious;
And if I indulge in a bite at a bulge,
Let's hope you won't think me too vicious.

Composed by Dylan Thomas at age eleven

EILEEN MYLES

The Irony of the Leash

Life is a plot to make me move.
I fill its forms, an unwitting
crayon
I am prey to the materials
of me, combinations
create me into something
else, civilization's inventions
numb me, placate me
carry me around. I
am no better than a dog.
My terms are not bark
and howl
but I often get drunk and raucous,
often I need to get
laid so bad I imagine my
howls lighting up the neighborhood
pasting rings
around the moon.
As a child I was very in love
with the stars. As a human
a victim of my perceptions
it is natural that I should love
light and as a passive dreamer
it is natural that I should be attracted

to the most distant inaccessible
light. What do you make of
this. Friend? I need the reassurance
of human voices so I live with
a phone or I go out and seek
my friends. Now they are always
different, these people
who
happen to be moved by the same
music as me, whose
faces I like, good voices,
I can recognize the oncoming footsteps
of a person I like. In this
I am little better than a dog.
Sometimes I go to the movies and I
sit in the dark. Leaving the light
and relishing the movements
of images occurring
in another time, bright
and pretty, and though I know
very well,
(as I paid my 1.50 and came
in here and chose a seat
a decision based on the condition
of my eyesight and my place
in society
I may sit in the front or

the back, am I old,
am I young ...)
I know very well that this movie is not
real, yet I am often
in the grips of fears more real
than those my own life throws up
for my unwilling complicity
and I am visibly shaken, often
nearly screaming with fright
and revulsion ...
yet I know it is not real.
Movies have caused me to become
an artist. I guess I simply
believe that life is not
enough. I spin dreams
of the quotidian out of words I
could not help but choose.
They reflect my educational background,
the economic situation of
my parents and the countries
their parents came from. My words
are also chemical reflections:
metabolically I am either fast or
slow, like short words or
long ones, sometimes I
like words which clack hard against
each other like a line of

wooden trains. Sometimes
I wish my words would meld
to a single glowing plastic tube slightly
defying time. I write
quite a bit,
I no longer believe in religion
but find writing an admirable
substitute,
I don't particularly believe in art
but I know that unless there is
something I do which is
at least as artificial and snide
and self-perpetuating
...
well then I would have to find
someone else who
had that sort of handle
on things and hold onto him
for dear life.
I would be less than a dog.
I think it's important to have
your own grip on
things, however
that works and then you should
pursue that and spend the
rest of the time
doing the ordinary.

Exactly like a dog. Dogs
are friendly creatures unless
they've been mistreated.
They like to eat and run around.
They neither drink nor smoke
nor take drugs. They are perfect.
They mate freely
whenever they have the urge.
They piss and shit according to
their needs, often they appear
to be smiling but of course
they are always happy.
Interestingly enough,
it is quite popular, particularly
in the city in which I live,
to own a dog, to walk him on a
leash
morning noon and night, people
with
families have dogs and they add
to the general abundant chaos
of the houschold,
people
who live alone own dogs. For
protection, regularity and
the general sense of owning a friend.

People
love their dogs and undoubtedly
their dogs love them. Though
they are faithless and impersonal.
They love their owners because
they feed them, stroke them,
bring them outside to run around,
if a dog gets injured
its owner will take it to a doctor or
a clinic, depending on the economic
situation of the owner.
Dogs do not believe in God or Art.
Intrinsically they have a grip
on things.
I unfortunately do not. I sit
here with a bottle of beer, a cigarette
and my latest poem, The Irony of the Leash.

August 6

LINDA PASTAN

The New Dog

Into the gravity of my life,
the serious ceremonies
of polish and paper
and pen, has come

this manic animal
whose innocent disruptions
make nonsense
of my old simplicities –

as if I needed him
to prove again that after
all the careful planning,
anything can happen.

WILLIAM SHAKESPEARE

from The Two Gentlemen of Verona

When a man's servant shall play the cur with him,
look you, it goes hard: one that I brought up of a
puppy; one that I saved from drowning, when three
or four of his blind brothers and sisters went to it.
I have taught him, even as one would say precisely,
'thus I would teach a dog.' I was sent to deliver him
as a present to Mistress Silvia from my master; and I
came no sooner into the dining-chamber but he steps
me to her trencher and steals her capon's leg: O, 'tis
a foul thing when a cur cannot keep himself in all
companies! I would have, as one should say, one that
takes upon him to be a dog indeed, to be, as it were,
a dog at all things. If I had not had more wit than he,
to take a fault upon me that he did, I think verily he
had been hanged for't; sure as I live, he had suffered
for't; you shall judge. He thrusts me himself into the
company of three or four gentlemanlike dogs under
the duke's table: he had not been there – bless the
mark! – a pissing while, but all the chamber smelt
him. 'Out with the dog!' says one: 'What cur is that?'
says another: 'Whip him out' says the third: 'Hang
him up' says the duke. I, having been acquainted
with the smell before, knew it was Crab, and goes
me to the fellow that whips the dogs: 'Friend,'

quoth I, 'you mean to whip the dog?' 'Ay, marry, do I,' quoth he. 'You do him the more wrong,' quoth I; ''twas I did the thing you wot of.' He makes me no more ado, but whips me out of the chamber. How many masters would do this for his servant? Nay, I'll be sworn, I have sat in the stocks for puddings he hath stolen, otherwise he had been executed; I have stood on the pillory for geese he hath killed, otherwise he had suffered for't. Thou thinkest not of this now. Nay, I remember the trick you served me when I took my leave of Madam Silvia: did not I bid thee still mark me and do as I do? when didst thou see me heave up my leg and make water against a gentlewoman's farthingale? didst thou ever see me do such a trick?

WILLIAM WORDSWORTH

Fidelity

A barking sound the Shepherd hears,
A cry as of a dog or fox;
He halts – and searches with his eyes
Among the scattered rocks:
And now at distance can discern
A stirring in a brake of fern;
And instantly a dog is seen,
Glancing through that covert green.

The Dog is not of mountain breed;
Its motions, too, are wild and shy;
With something, as the Shepherd thinks,
Unusual in its cry:
Nor is there any one in sight
All round, in hollow or on height;
Nor shout, nor whistle strikes his ear;
What is the creature doing here?

It was a cove, a huge recess,
That keeps, till June, December's snow;
A lofty precipice in front,
A silent tarn below!
Far in the bosom of Helvellyn,
Remote from public road or dwelling,

Pathway, or cultivated land;
From trace of human foot or hand.

There sometimes doth a leaping fish
Send through the tarn a lonely cheer;
The crags repeat the raven's croak,
In symphony austere;
Thither the rainbow comes – the cloud –
And mists that spread the flying shroud;
And sunbeams; and the sounding blast,
That, if it could, would hurry past;
But that enormous barrier holds it fast.

Not free from boding thoughts, a while
The Shepherd stood; then makes his way
O'er rocks and stones, following the Dog
As quickly as he may;
Nor far had gone before he found
A human skeleton on the ground;
The appalled Discoverer with a sigh
Looks round, to learn the history.

From those abrupt and perilous rocks
The Man had fallen, that place of fear!
At length upon the Shepherd's mind
It breaks, and all is clear:

He instantly recalled the name,
And who he was, and whence he came;
Remembered, too, the very day
On which the Traveller passed this way.

But hear a wonder, for whose sake
This lamentable tale I tell!
A lasting monument of words
This wonder merits well.
The Dog, which still was hovering nigh,
Repeating the same timid cry,
This Dog, had been through three months' space
A dweller in that savage place.

Yes, proof was plain that, since the day
When this ill-fated Traveller died,
The Dog had watched about the spot,
Or by his master's side:
How nourished here through such long time
He knows, who gave that love sublime;
And gave that strength of feeling, great
Above all human estimate!

WILLIAM DICKEY

Hope

At the foot of the stairs
my black dog sits;
in his body,
out of his wits.

On the other side
of the shut front door
there's a female dog
he's nervous for.

She's the whole size
of his mind – immense.
Hope ruling him
past sense.

EMILY DICKINSON

I Started Early—Took My Dog

I started Early—Took my Dog—
And visited the Sea—
The Mermaids in the Basement
Came out to look at me—

And Frigates—in the Upper Floor
Extended Hempen Hands—
Presuming Me to be a Mouse—
Aground—upon the Sands—

But no Man moved Me—till the Tide
Went past my simple Shoe—
And past my Apron—and my Belt
And past my Bodice—too—

And made as He would eat me up—
As wholly as a Dew
Upon a Dandelion's Sleeve—
And then—I started—too—

And He—He followed—close behind—
I felt His Silver Heel
Upon my Ankle—Then my Shoes
Would overflow with Pearl—

Until We met the Solid Town—
No One He seemed to know—
And bowing—with a Mighty look—
At me—The Sea withdrew—

JONATHAN SWIFT

Advice to a Dog Painter

Happiest of the spaniel race,
Painter, with thy colors grace,
Draw his forehead large and high,
Draw his blue and humid eye;
Draw his neck, so smooth and round,
Little neck with ribands bound;
And the musely swelling breast
Where the Loves and Graces rest;
And the spreading, even back,
Soft, and sleek, and glossy black;
And the tail that gently twines,
Like the tendrils of the vines;
And the silky twisted hair,
Shadowing thick the velvet ear;
Velvet ears which, hanging low,
O'er the veiny temples flow.

Over and Over Tune

You could grow into it,
that sense of living like a dog,
loyal to being on your own in the fur of your skin,
able to exist only for the sake of existing.

Nothing inside your head lasting long enough for
you to hold onto,
you watch your own thoughts leap across your own
synapses and disappear –
small boats in a wind,
    fliers in all that blue,
        the swish of an arm backed with feathers,
a dress talking in a corner,
        and then poof,
    your mind clean as a dog's,
your body big as the world,
    important with accident –
        blood or a limp, fur and paws.

You swell into survival,
    you take up the whole day,
you're all there is,
    everything else is
not you, is every passing glint, is

shadows brought to you by wind,
        passing into a bird's cheep, replaced by a
            rabbit skittering across a yard,
a void you yourself fall into.

You could make this beautiful,
    but you don't need to,
living is this fleshy side of the bone,
    going on is this medicinal smell of the sun –
        no dog ever tires of seeing his life

keep showing up at the back door
even as a rotting bone with a bad smell;
feet tottering, he dreams of it,
wakes and licks no matter what.

LOUIS MACNEICE

Dogs in the Park

The precise yet furtive etiquette of dogs
Makes them ignore the whistle while they talk
In circles round each other, one-man bonds
Deferred in pauses of this man-made walk
To open vistas to a past of packs
That raven round the stuccoed terraces
And scavenge at the mouth of Stone Age caves;
What man proposes dog on his day disposes
In litter round both human and canine graves,
Then lifts his leg to wash the gravestones clean,
Better than Mortal Flowers
While simultaneously his eyes express
Apology and contempt; his master calls
And at the last and sidelong he returns,
Part heretic, part hack, and jumps and crawls
And fumbles to communicate and fails.
And then they leave the park, the leads are snapped
On to the spiky collars, the tails wag
For no known reason and the ears are pricked
To search through legendary copse and crag
For legendary creatures doomed to die
Even as they, the dogs, were doomed to live.

Geist's Grave

FOUR years! – and didst thou stay above
The ground, which hides thee now, but four?
And all that life, and all that love,
Were crowded, Geist! into no more?

Only four years those winning ways,
Which make me for thy presence yearn,
Call'd us to pet thee or to praise,
Dear little friend! at every turn?

That loving heart, that patient soul,
Had they indeed no longer span,
To run their course, and reach their goal,
And read their homily to man?

That liquid, melancholy eye,
From whose pathetic, soul-fed springs
Seem'd urging the Virgilian cry,
The sense of tears in mortal things –

That steadfast, mournful strain, consol'd
By spirits gloriously gay,
And temper of heroic mould –
What, was four years their whole short day?

Yes, only four! – and not the course
Of all the centuries yet to come,
And not the infinite resource
Of Nature, with her countless sum

Of figures, with her fulness vast
Of new creation evermore,
Can ever quite repeat the past,
Or just thy little self restore.

Stern law of every mortal lot!
Which man, proud man, finds hard to bear,
And builds himself I know not what
Of second life I know not where.

But thou, when struck thine hour to go,
On us, who stood despondent by,
A meek last glance of love didst throw,
And humbly lay thee down to die.

Yet would we keep thee in our heart –
Would fix our favorite on the scene,
Nor let thee utterly depart
And be as if thou ne'er hadst been.

And so there rise these lines of verse
On lips that rarely form them now;
While to each other we rehearse:
Such ways, such arts, such looks hadst thou!

We stroke thy broad brown paws again,
We bid thee to thy vacant chair,
We greet thee by the window-pane,
We hear thy scuffle on the stair.

We see the flaps of thy large ears
Quick rais'd to ask which way we go;
Crossing the frozen lake, appears
Thy small black figure on the snow!

Nor to us only art thou dear
Who mourn thee in thine English home;
Thou hast thine absent master's tear,
Dropp'd by the far Australian foam.

Thy memory lasts both here and there,
And thou shalt live as long as we.
And after that – thou dost not care!
In us was all the world to thee.

Yet, fondly zealous for thy fame,
Even to a date beyond our own
We strive to carry down thy name,
By mounded turf, and graven stone.

We lay thee, close within our reach,
Here, where the grass is smooth and warm,
Between the holly and the beech,
Where oft we watch'd thy couchant form,

Asleep, yet lending half an ear
To travellers on the Portsmouth road; –
There build we thee, O guardian dear,
Mark'd with a stone, thy last abode!

Then some, who through this garden pass,
When we too, like thyself, are clay,
Shall see thy grave upon the grass,
And stop before the stone, and say:

People who lived here long ago
Did by this stone, it seems, intend
To name for future times to know
The dachs-hound, Geist, their little friend.

Scroppo's Dog

In the early morning, past the shut houses,
past the harbor shut in fog, I walk free and
single. It is summer – that's lucky. The whole
day is mine. At the end of our village I stop
to greet Scroppo's dog, whose chain is wrapped
around a large dusty boulder. His black coat
is gray, from crouching every day in the gravel
of Scroppo's yard – a yard by a scrap-filled pond,
where Scroppo deals in wrecked cars and car parts.
I guess he gets them from crashes on the
    expressway,
or from abandoned junks he loots by the roadside.
I don't know the name of Scroppo's dog.
    I remember
him, years ago, as a big fierce-looking pup.
It may have been his first day chained there,
or shortly after, that he first greeted me:
his eyes big nuggets shooting orange sparks, his
red tongue rippling out between clean fangs –
fangs as white as lilies of the valley that bloom
in a leafy border by Scroppo's weathered porch.
It was late May, as now, when with sudden joyful
bark, black fur erect and gleaming, the dog
rushed toward me – but was stopped by his chain,

a chain then bright and new. I would have met
and stroked him, but didn't dare get near him,
in his strangled frenzy – in his unbelief –
that something at his throat cut short
his coming, going, leaping, circling, running –
something he couldn't bite through, tripped him:
he could go only so far: to the trash in the weeds
at the end of the driveway, to the edge
of the oily, broken cement in back, where Scroppo's
muddy flatbed truck stands at night.
Now, as I walk toward him, the dog growls,
then cowers back. He is old and fat and dirty,
and his eyes spit equal hate and fear.
He knows exactly how far he can strain
from the rock and the wrapped chain. There's
a trench in a circle in the oily dirt his paws
have dug. Day and weeks and months and years
of summer heat and winter cold have been survived
within the radius of that chain.
Scroppo's dog knows me, and wants to come and
touch. At the same time, his duty to expel
the intruder makes him bare his teeth and
bristle. He pounds his matted tail, he snarls
while cringing, alternately stretched toward me
and springs back. His bark, husky and cracked,
crossing the boundary of the cove.
I've never touched Scroppo's dog, and his

yearning tongue has never licked me. Yet, we
know each other well. Subject to the seasons'
extremes, confined to the limits of our yard,
early fettered by an obscure master in whose
power we bask, bones grow frail while steel
thickens; while rock fattens, passions and
senses pale. Scroppo's dog sniffs dust.
He sleeps a lot. My nose grown blunt, I need
to remember the salty damp of the air's taste
on summer mornings, first snowfall's freshness,
the smoke of burning leaves. Each midday,
when the firehouse whistle blows, a duet
of keen, weird howls is heard, as, at the steep
edge of hopelessness, with muzzle pointed,
earls flat, eyes shut, Scroppo's dog forlornly
yodels in time to the village siren sounding noon.

The grass is wet on the hill.
The sky has no end.
For the dog who waits for his mistress,
Madge, noon comes again.

Beyond the hills, a master is
who knows our secret names.
With bell and bones, he'll call us home,
winter, fall or spring.

GEOFFREY CHAUCER

from *The Book of the Duchess*

... I was go walked fro my tree,
And as I wente, ther cam by me
A whelp, that fauned me as I stood,
That hadde y-folowed, and koude no good.
Hit com and creep to me as lowe,
Right as hit hadde me y-knowe,
Hild doun his heed and joyned his eres,
And leyde al smothe doun his heres.
I wolde han caught hit, and anoon
Hit fledde, and was fro me goon;
And I him folwed, and hit forth wente
Doun by a floury grene wente
Ful thikke of gras, ful softe and swete,
With floures fele, faire under fete,
And litel used, hit seemed thus;
For bothe Flora and Zephirus,
They two that make floures growe,
Had mad hir dwelling ther, I trowe;
For hit was, on to beholde,
As thogh the erthe envye wolde
To be gayer than the heven,
To have mo floures, swiche seven
As in the welken sterres be.

Hit had forgete the povertee
That winter, through his colde morwes,
Had mad hit suffren, and his sorwes;
Al was forgeten, and that was sene.
For al the wode was waxen grene,
Swetnesse of dewe had mad it waxe.

Hit is no need eek for to axe
Wher ther were many grene greves,
Or thikke of trees, so ful of leves;
And every tree stood by himselve
Fro other wel ten foot or twelve.
So grete trees, so huge of strengthe,
Of fourty or fifty fadme lengthe,
Clene withoute bough or stikke,
With croppes brode, and eek as thikke –
They were nat an inche asonder –
That hit was shadwe overal under;
And many an hert and many an hynde
Was both before me and bihinde.
Of founes, soures, bukkes, does
Was ful the wode, and many roes,
And many squirelles that sete
Ful hye upon the trees, and ete,
And in hir maner made festes.
Shortly, hit was so ful of bestes,
That thogh Argus, the noble countour,

Sete to rekene in his countour,
And rekene with his figures ten –
For by tho figures mowe al ken,
If they be crafty, rekene and noumbre,
And telle of every thing the noumbre –
Yet shulde he fayle to rekene even
The wondres, me mette in my sweven.

RUDYARD KIPLING

The Power of the Dog

There is sorrow enough in the natural way
From men and women to fill our day;
And when we are certain of sorrow in store,
Why do we always arrange for more?
Brothers and Sisters, I bid you beware
Of giving your heart to a dog to tear.

Buy a pup and your money will buy
Love unflinching that cannot lie –
Perfect passion and worship fed
By a kick in the ribs or a pat on the head.
Nevertheless it is hardly fair
To risk your heart for a dog to tear.

When the fourteen years which Nature permits
Are closing in asthma, or tumour, or fits,
And the vet's unspoken prescription runs
To lethal chambers or loaded guns,
Then you will find – it's your own affair –
But ... you've given your heart for a dog to tear.

When the body that lived at your single will,
With its whimper of welcome, is stilled (how still!);
When the spirit that answered your every mood

Is gone – wherever it goes – for good,
You will discover how much you care,
And will give your heart for the dog to tear.

We've sorrow enough in the natural way,
When it comes to burying Christian clay.
Our loves are not given, but only lent,
At compound interest of cent per cent.
Though it is not always the case, I believe,
That the longer we've kept 'em, the more
    do we grieve:
For, when debts are payable, right or wrong,
A short-time loan is as bad as a long –
So why in Heaven (before we are there)
Should we give our hearts to a dog to tear?

DAVID BAKER

Mongrel Heart

Up the dog bounds to the window, baying
　　like a basset his doleful, tearing sounds
　　　　from the belly, as if mourning a dead king,

and now he's howling like a beagle – yips, brays,
　　gagging growls – and scratching the sill
　　　　paintless,
　　　　　　that's how much he's missed you, the two
　　　　　　　　of you,

both of you, mother and daughter, my wife
　　and child. All week he's curled at my feet,
　　　　warming himself and me watching more TV,

or wandered the lonely rooms, my dog shadow,
　　who like a poodle now hops, amped-up windup
　　　　maniac yo-yo with matted curls and snot nose

smearing the panes, having heard another car
　　like yours taking its grinding turn down
　　　　our block, or a school bus, or bird-squawk,

that's how much he's missed you, good dog,
　　companion dog, dog-of-all-types, most
　　　　excellent dog
　　　　　　I told you once and for all we should never get.

ANNE KINGSMILL FINCH

The Dog And His Master

No better Dog e'er kept his Master's Door
Than honest Snarl, who spar'd nor Rich nor Poor;
But gave the Alarm, when any one drew nigh,
Nor let pretended Friends pass fearless by:
For which reprov'd, as better Fed than Taught,
He rightly thus expostulates the Fault.

To keep the House from Rascals was my Charge;
The Task was great, and the Commission large.
Nor did your Worship e'er declare your Mind,
That to the begging Crew it was confin'd;
Who shrink an Arm, or prop an able Knee,
Or turn up Eyes, till they're not seen, nor see.
To Thieves, who know the Penalty of Stealth,
And fairly stake their Necks against your Wealth,
These are the known Delinquents of the Times,
And Whips and Tyburn testify their Crimes.

But since to Me there was by Nature lent
An exquisite Discerning by the Scent;
I trace a Flatt'rer, when he fawns and leers,
A rallying Wit, when he commends and jeers:
The greedy Parasite I grudging note,
Who praises the good Bits, that oil his Throat;

I mark the Lady, you so fondly toast,
That plays your Gold, when all her own is lost:
The Knave, who fences your Estate by Law,
Yet still reserves an undermining Flaw.
These and a thousand more, which I cou'd tell,
Provoke my Growling, and offend my Smell.

If Feeling Isn't In It

Dogs will also lick your face if you let them.
Their bodies will shiver with happiness.
A simple walk in the park is just about
the height of contentment for them, followed
by a bowl of food, a bowl of water,
a place to curl up and sleep. Someone
to scratch them where they can't reach
and smooth their foreheads and talk to them.
Dogs also have a natural dislike of mailmen
and other bringers of bad news and will
bite them on your behalf. Dogs can smell
fear and also love with perfect accuracy.
There is no use pretending with them.
Nor do they pretend. If a dog is happy
or sad or nervous or bored or ashamed
or sunk in contemplation, everybody knows it.
They make no secret of themselves.
You can even tell what they're dreaming about
by the way their legs jerk and try to run
on the slippery ground of sleep.
Nor are they given to pretentious self-importance.
They don't try to impress you with how serious
or sensitive they are. They just feel everything
full blast. Everything is off the charts

with them. More than once I've seen a dog
waiting for its owner outside a café
practically implode with worry. 'Oh, God,
what if she doesn't come back this time?
What will I do? Who will take care of me?
I loved her so much and now she's gone
and I'm tied to a post surrounded by people
who don't look or smell or sound like her at all.'
And when she does come, what a flurry
of commotion, what a chorus of yelping
and cooing and leaps straight up into the air!
It's almost unbearable, this sudden
fullness after such total loss, to see
the world made whole again by a hand
on the shoulder and a voice like no other.

To the Quarry and Back

White hail pelting the frozen bog,
I'm stuck in the first line of January,
following my host's dog
on his walk through the stone century,
around the quarry, slices of marble and mud,
past a herd of miners exhaling smoke,
past a barn smelling of merde,
and back to where I'm stuck and broke.
The fucking dog barks at the night,
mad at the stars all his life and then again.
I rethink kicking him out,
but being cool, I let him in.

TRANSLATED BY **ALEXANDER POPE**

Argus, from *The Odyssey*

When wise Ulysses, from his native coast
Long kept by wars, and long by tempests toss'd,
Arrived at last, poor, old, disguised, alone,
To all his friends, and ev'n his Queen unknown,
Changed as he was, with age, and toils, and cares,
Furrow'd his rev'rend face, and white his hairs,
In his own palace forc'd to ask his bread,
Scorn'd by those slaves his former bounty fed,
Forgot of all his own domestic crew,
The faithful Dog alone his rightful master knew!

Unfed, unhous'd, neglected, on the clay
Like an old servant now cashier'd, he lay;
Touch'd with resentment of ungrateful man,
And longing to behold his ancient lord again.
Him when he saw he rose, and crawl'd to meet,
('Twas all he could) and fawn'd and kiss'd his feet,
Seiz'd with dumb joy; then falling by his side,
Own'd his returning lord, look'd up, and died!

WILLIAM COWPER

The Dog and The Waterlily
(No Fable)

The noon was shady, and soft airs
    Swept Ouse's silent tide,
When, 'scap'd from literary cares,
    I wander'd on his side.

My spaniel, prettiest of his race,
    And high in pedigree,
(Two nymphs, adorned with ev'ry grace,
    That spaniel found for me)

Now wanton'd lost in flags and reeds,
    Now starting into sight
Pursued the swallow o'er the meads
    With scarce a slower flight.

It was the time when Ouse display'd
    His lilies newly blown;
Their beauties I intent survey'd,
    And one I wish'd my own.

With cane extended far I sought
    To steer it close to land;
But still the prize, though nearly caught,
    Escap'd my eager hand.

Beau marked my unsuccessful pains
    With fixt consid'rate face,
And puzzling set his puppy brains
    To comprehend the case.

But with a chirrup clear and strong,
    Dispersing all his dream,
I thence withdrew, and follow'd long
    The windings of the stream.

My ramble finished, I return'd.
    Beau trotting far before
The floating wreath again discern'd,
    And plunging left the shore.

I saw him with that lily cropp'd
    Impatient swim to meet
My quick approach, and soon he dropp'd
    The treasure at my feet.

Charm'd with the sight, the world, I cried,
    Shall hear of this thy deed,
My dog shall mortify the pride
    Of man's superior breed;

But, chief, myself I will enjoin,
    Awake at duty's call,
To show a love as prompt as thine
    To Him who gives me all.

DENISE LEVERTOV

The Dog of Art

That dog with daisies for eyes
who flashes forth
flame of his very self at every bark
is the Dog of Art.
Worked in wool, his blind eyes
look inward to caverns and jewels
which they see perfectly,
and his voice
measures forth the treasure
in music sharp and loud,
sharp and bright,
bright flaming barks,
and growling smoky soft, the Dog
of Art turns to the world
the quietness of his eyes.

Sources

ANDRÉ ALEXIS, 'Running through the grey-eyed dawn ...' from *Fifteen Dogs*, Serpent's Tail. Copyright © 2015 by André Alexis.

DAVID BAKER, 'Mongrel Heart' from the *Southeast Review*, Vol. 23, No. 2. Copyright © 2005 by David Baker.

ELIZABETH BISHOP, 'Pink Dog' from *Complete Poems*, Chatto & Windus. Copyright © 2004 by The Alice H. Methfessel Trust.

JOHN BREHM, 'If Feeling Isn't in It' from *Sea of Faith*, University of Wisconsin Press. Copyright © 2004 by John Brehm.

IOANNA CARLSEN, 'Over and Over Tune' from *Poetry*. Copyright © 2001 by Ioanna Carlsen.

MARCHETTE CHUTE, 'My Dog', source unknown.

CECIL DAY-LEWIS, 'Sheepdog Trials in Hyde Park' from *The Complete Poems*, Vintage. Copyright © by Cecil Day-Lewis, 2012.

DOROTHY PARKER, 'Verse for a Certain Dog' from *The Complete Poems Of Dorothy Parker* by Dorothy Parker. Copyright © 1999 by The National Association for the Advancement of Colored People. Reprinted by permission of Penguin Books, an imprint of Penguin Publishing Group, a division of Penguin Random House LLC. All rights reserved.

LINDA PASTAN, 'The New Dog' from *A Dog Runs Through It*, W. W. Norton, 2018.

IRENE RUTHERFORD MCLEOD, 'Lone Dog' from *Songs to Save a Soul*, Chatto & Windus, 1916.

SIEGFRIED SASSOON, 'Man and Dog' from *Collected Poems*. Copyright © by Siegfried Sassoon, reprinted by kind permission of the Estate of George Sassoon.

STEVIE SMITH, 'O Pug!' from *Collected Poems of Stevie Smith*. Copyright © 1972 by Stevie Smith.

VINCENT STARRETT, 'Oracle of the Dog' from *Collected Poems: Vincent Starrett*. Copyright © 2017 by The Battered Silicon Dispatch Box.

MAY SWENSON, 'Scroppo's Dog' from *Nature*. Copyright © 1994 by the Literary Estate of May Swenson.

DYLAN THOMAS, 'The Song of the Mischievous Dog' from *The Poems of Dylan Thomas*. Copyright © 1957 by The Trustees for the copyrights of Dylan Thomas. Composed by Dylan Thomas at age eleven.

PAUL ZIMMER, 'Dog Music' from *Crossing to Sunlight: Revisited*, University of Georgia Press. Copyright © 2017 by Paul Zimmer.